A DOSE OF MOTIVATION

The Cure to Any Entrepreneur Struggle

Kimberly Genwright-Fulton

Kimberly Genwright-Fulton

Copyright © 2016 Kimberly Genwright-Fulton
All rights reserved.

ISBN: 1535559160
ISBN-13: 9781535559164

CONTENTS

	Introduction	6
1.	Daily Dose: Life	11
2.	Daily Dose: Encouragement In Your Tiredness	13
3.	Daily Dose: Little Pick Me Up	15
4.	Daily Dose: The Many Hats	18
5.	Daily Dose: Breaking Bread	20
6.	Daily Dose: How Professional Are You	22
7.	Daily Dose: Making An Impact	24
8.	Daily Dose: Threatened By Your Reflection	26
9.	Daily Dose: The Rain	28
10.	Daily Dose: Your Reliable Source	30
11.	Daily Dose: Time For A Change	32
12.	Daily Dose: What Do You See	34
13.	Daily Dose: Reality Check	37
14.	Daily Dose: The Resolution	39
15.	Daily Dose: Your Net Worth	41
16.	Daily Dose: Renew	43
17.	Daily Dose: Which Way Are You Headed?	45
18.	Daily Dose: The Beginning	47
19.	Daily Dose: The Mission	49

20. Daily Dose: The Spotlight   **51**

21. Daily Dose: The Success   **53**

22. Questions For Self-Evaluation   **55**

                  Acknowledgements   **59**

INTRODUCTION

As a young girl, I can remember watching on television the men and women in major metropolitan areas such as New York City and Washington, D.C. They were walking around with their briefcases. Seeing these images inspired me. I would find myself saying, "When I get older this is what I am going to do." Now mind you, I had no idea what was in the briefcase or what they were doing, but it looked important. As I sit and reflect now, it is mind blowing on how I was carried away by the look of it, not knowing how hard they were working day in and out.

    The reason I am pointing this out is because we all have a passion or desire centered on something we would like to achieve. Something catches our attention and no matter how we try to look past it, it always has a way of coming back into our remembrance. I decided to follow the light that popped in my head a couple of years ago. I decided to achieve my goals of becoming an entrepreneur, small business coach and author.

    Not doing this for a show of approval, I wanted to secure my future and lend a helping hand to those in need of my services. My desire is to help someone with pursuing his or her goals. I get joy when I hear someone wanting to change their lifestyle for the better whether it is going into business for themselves or investing in an opportunity. The keywords found on any journey of entrepreneurship are empowerment, motivation and determination. Sometimes people are so broken, all they need is someone to help them put back the pieces. Sometimes our dreams are crushed because of what others perceive are our limitations or incapability.

    I can remember a couple of years ago traveling out of town with a relative, enjoying a new environment and admiring what the city had to offer, but sadly getting depressed about coming back to a place I called home, Marion County. This was not only my birthplace, but the place where I grew up with all of my hopes and dreams. This place had become a ghost town. Workers began being laid off by their employers. Once the layoffs began, job closings quickly followed. For most of these workers, this was the only job they had ever known. The truth of the matter is this was all they were taught.

    I have heard many people say if you have a job keep it. This is fine, but what happens when you give your all to a company with very little time for yourself and all of a sudden it's gone? What do you do then? What is your next move? This question has left many puzzled. The amazing thing is some of the people knew how to run and operate the company better than their management. With so much talent and capability, performing your own actions in the end, could be the establishment of your empire. There are many skillful people out here that need the teaching and understanding of becoming an entrepreneur. Never under estimate yourself. You can do it if you put your mind to it.

If you are reading this, I pray you will believe in yourself enough to invest in yourself. I may not be where I want to be, but I know that I am well on my way because of the potential that lies within me. Every morning I stare at the image of who could be the next spokesman for the magazine *Entrepreneur*. I could grace the cover and discuss my many accomplishments, but so can you.

Let's say your hobby is styling hair. Why not get paid for your passion and open a salon? Are you good at fixing cars? Why not open a car repair shop? Some people are knowledgeable in certain areas and it is my job to coach them into taking that one step forward.

There are many resources available to give you the basics, but it has to come from within. It has to be a desire more than a want. A lot of times we are afraid of the responsibilities and stress that comes with having our own business. Yes, there are times when it is not going to be easy, but who says you have to do it alone? You will be amazed at the number of volunteers who have crossed there T's, dotted there I's and are willing to help in any way possible.

On this journey, I realized that having one person believe in me made the difference in my life. Hearing the words, "You can do it," put me in a position to conquer. We are all blessed, but some of us don't realize how blessed we are. Many doors are opening where we can walk in and take control over our life to provide a better future for ourselves and our family. Grants are available for our usage and loans that will allow us in schools and universities. Some are free. Why miss the opportunity to freshen your skills. Having a little knowledge puts us in places and positions we only dream about. Why would you let all of your talent go to waste? Why not invest in yourself? All you need is a plan, determination, and a goal. The best thing about it is, these are free. You don't have to have a certain background or six degrees; all you need is a willing mind.

I want you to be empowered and inspired. I have the faith that anyone can do anything they put their minds too. It doesn't matter how young or old you are, you can become your own boss and enjoy the freedom this life brings. I have heard many people complain about how much they hate their jobs and the low salary. If you are one of those people, my question is what are you doing about it? Are you going to settle for that low salary rate, or, are you going to equip yourself with the ability to change your circumstances? The choice is yours. Think of it this way, wouldn't you love the opportunity to wake up and look forward to what your daily schedule beholds? I know I would.

Take the time now to secure your future. Have a backup plan in case your current one fails. If you aren't sure why you should, consider attending some workshops, seminars, or self-enrichment courses to direct you on the right path and give you the knowledge you need to achieve your desires. If transportation is a problem, consider an online course that can give you the education needed to launch your ideal career. Check your local papers for events that may advertise business opportunities or to read daily articles that speak-to you. Once you have made a decision on which educational or career path to choose, consult with an admissions counselor, business owner, or consultant and inquire about their journey.

Don't be afraid to trust someone else with your goals or vision. There is always someone willing to listen and share their experiences. I find myself becoming a bookworm. I'm always searching and looking for more knowledge in case I missed something. In addition to this, it is important to remain current and stay relevant. You can never get enough of learning. You never know, you might become the president one day. I think I'll remain true to my current path and let our current president manage that task, but never say never. You can only go as high as you allow yourself. Remember the sky is the limit. I have had to tell myself this every day.

The day I decided to begin my journey as a writer was when I started taking care of my mother who became ill in 2005. I can remember that day as if it was yesterday. It was a Saturday evening and she was babysitting her grandkids. On that evening I had some plans to step out for a while, but I noticed she wasn't as energetic as she usually was when they were visiting with her. She started mentioning that she had a slight headache and wasn't feeling too well. I would not have ever imagined she was having a stroke. I figured it was stress-related or tension. I cancelled my plans and stayed at the house with her.

Later on that evening she went to the restroom and as she was exiting she yelled out that she couldn't walk. I am assuming this is the point of when the stroke occurred. We took her to the emergency room and the doctors examined her and ruled out that she had suffered a stroke. This is one of the last words you would want to hear regarding a parent or any loved one. My mother experienced short-term memory loss. The stroke damaged her brain cells while causing her left side to become weak. I remained in the home with her after the hospital stay and rehabilitation period to provide care. I felt as if it was my duty and job as her daughter to do what I know she would have done for me. It was especially hard not being able to do most of the things that I use to by going out with my friends, going away for a weekend, things of that sort. I did what I had to, and complaining was not going to help the situation.

Four years later, I married a wonderful man and I moved to Columbia, South Carolina, with my husband. We decided to bring my mother along to live with us. I must pause and give my husband kudos. He has been an outstanding support system and patient with my mom and I. I believe most men would not stand by your side when you are caring for a loved one because it is stressful and tries your patience. I am very thankful. My family and I have lived in Columbia since 2010. Upon my arrival, I was able to get a work-from-home job as an employee of a call center. It was a blessing because it allowed me to care for my mom and contribute financially to the household. I worked there for three years. During this same time, I picked up writing small articles for Examiner.com in the Small Business section. In 2010, I decided to work on reconciling with my father and close the gap that existed between us. We talked numerous times and I enjoyed every conversation. June 2013, my mother unfortunately suffered another mini stroke. It was detected in a small spot in the back of her brain by the MRI. We were devastated. I begin wondering how this could happen when her blood sugar levels had been great, no salt intake and blood pressure normal. It made me feel as if I did something wrong. Her physician calmed my anxiety by stating it wasn't anything I could have done.

He mentioned that although everything was normal and actually great, sometimes matters happen beyond our control. After my mother's hospital stay, she was able to get the assistance needed to recover. Once my mother's health and wellness was under control, life dealt another blow as my father was diagnosed with lung cancer. He passed away November 2013. Shortly thereafter, I began writing more realizing that there is no time like the present to complete the task you set out to do because time waits for no one. I could sit around, complain and feel sorry for myself that things aren't the way I intended, but what is the point of that.

Why not push and focus more on my dreams? I may not ever have another chance. My dreams and goals started at a young age, in my mind at the age I am now those dreams and goals needed to be met. I always wanted a career, something that belonged to me. This isn't anything against working for someone else, but time and other extenuating circumstances has not permitted me to, so I feel that God has something bigger and better for me, and the only way I will receive it is if I go after it. There have been times when it seemed as if friends had deserted me, but it was all predestined by God to allow me to focus more on Him to get to where I am going now. I didn't fully understand it then, but I do now.

My purpose for writing this book is to encourage anyone who feels as if you are at a standstill in pursing your goals, or you feel as if it can't happen for you. I am here to let you know you can do anything you put your mind too and there are no limits to what you can achieve. Regardless of the stumbling blocks in your way just know that God has a plan for your escape and with HIM ALL THINGS ARE POSSIBLE.

As you continue reading you will notice that the next few pages will consist of different journal entries I have written as I maintained my journey of becoming an entrepreneur. I have provided a starting point in the beginning of my writing, but now you get to venture out into my struggles, hurt and encouragement that I have built within myself to continue. I felt that sharing with you the many issues I faced will cause you to realize that this was written from my heart and experiences. It is not your typical self-help book. As you begin reading you will notice that my content was written based on my state of mind whether it was on a good or bad day. You will experience the stages I went through to commit myself to stay on my quest as an entrepreneur. Articles are included that will aid you in having a successful business. So again, I hope you will be able to believe and push yourself as I did. I am sure you will find something that will speak to your situation.

Daily Dose: Life

I have been in deep thought regarding my life. Life in and of itself can be stressful, but rewarding. The reward occurs with knowing who you are all the while making the most of it here on earth. I believe it is time for us to stop being broken over matters we can't change. Instead of dreading over issues we should focus on changing ourselves. Maybe if we changed our viewpoint, we will begin to harvest the favor. I know I have to make some custom changes to be able to grab onto what has been promised to me.

One of my goals is to empower others to seek their foundation. I admire those who are going after their goals in the face of rejection and disappointment. This assures me that they are determined to make their mark. If you are at a standstill, I invite you to reflect on your childhood. Back then the teacher would have us stand in front of the class and tell them what we wanted to be when we grew up. How many of you reading this book can say you are doing those things at this very moment? Well we all experienced this thing called life, and trust me it comes with a lot of ups and downs. It even prevents some of us from reaching our destination.

I know I fit this category well, but the good thing is it is never too late. Since I'm older I have a different mindset with entirely new concepts. My ideas are newer and fresher than ever before. If this describes you in any way, I know you can relate to what I am saying. Let's make this life better by conquering some of the giants that have been placed in our way. Regardless of your gender, the opportunities are there for you to take full advantage of. Today I woke up with a burst of good energy to get things done. I didn't want to sit around and wish someone would do it for me.

I realized that this is the season for overflow, the season to branch off into your calling. Get inspired. Pull out those talents and gifts and let's make the best of what we have. We are only here for a short period of time. Let's not waste it on something that is not going to help us in the long run. Believe it or not you do have some people who are rooting for you to achieve your goals.

Life does not always have to be hard. There can and will be lessons learned along the way. I ask that you seek God in everything you do. Trust me. He will give you that missing piece to the puzzle that is needed to make your dreams complete. My advice to you: stay encouraged, go after your dreams and enjoy life while you still can.

Just because some time has passed doesn't mean that it is over. Life is full of options you just need to choose one. Don't allow a time frame to persuade you that your time is up. The same goals you had back then can be your reality now.

Reflection:

_____

_____

_____

Daily Dose: Encouragement in Your Tiredness

It is amazing how God allows two individual paths to cross who are aiming for the same goal. A lot of times when we are trying to get to certain destinations we always find ourselves being thrown off of the path we are trying to get too. In some cases it makes us feel as if the quest is always harder for us than anyone else.

I often used to think I was the only one who experienced setbacks. I know it sounds crazy, but I am only speaking truth. I met someone who I was helping out with a job prospect. She wanted to befriend me on Facebook. Little did I know that she would be the motivation I needed to continue my writing journey. I discovered she had also written books while being a caregiver to her husband and in-laws. She and I shared things with each other that we both were going through. I was able to express things to her I knew she would understand.

As I was chatting with her, I found myself emotional as I began sharing my feelings. When she mentioned that I needed a break, something broke within me. I realized that for so long the reason for my setbacks in personal achievement was because I was tired. So much that I could not press through completing the tasks. I was so tired of my situation that my focus was on what I couldn't do.

In order to achieve any goal, you must have the will power to continue what you started. If you are only looking at your negatives you will always be miles away from your positives. My negatives were simply being tired and focusing on what someone else wasn't doing instead of accepting the role I played. My situation was a blessing and I didn't realize it. It allowed me to trust God to lay ahold of my desires. It allowed me to be determined to fulfill His destinies. It allowed me to be who I am today. I am a beautiful woman inside and out who can do anything she puts her mind too. I am smart, intelligent and a go-getter with a winning attitude designed and sealed with God's stamp of approval.

Someone needs to speak this within themselves. Make a mental note if you have too. Forget about your worries and take ahold of your future. Respect yourself enough to remove the boundaries you have placed over your life. Trust me. Removing those limitations will allow you to grab onto your blessings. Your blessing is having a wonderful future, living comfortably in knowing you stepped out on faith while still standing when the door was slammed in your face, when told you didn't get the job, or you were over qualified for the position.

Some of you don't realize the level of potential in you. Some of you who might not have finished high school or went to college may feel as if it is impossible for you, but that is not true you are only hindered by what you don't see. Once you begin to envision your greatness then you will be able to prevail in your success. Never speak doubt in your situation regardless of what is in your pocket speak prosperity and watch God bless you with tenfold.

Don't look at your weakness as a failure look at it as a step closer to your destination. Whatever you do don't give up remember you are fighting for a reason, and that reason is to win.

Reflection:

_____

_____

_____

Daily Dose: Little Pick Me Up

Today was one of those days where I was really struggling. I had to have a talk with myself. No, I am not crazy I just needed to give myself an extra boost. I had things I needed to do, but part of me wondered the point of it all. Have you ever felt this way? I was having a solo pity party.

Sometimes, I have to encourage myself to keep going. Even though I am trying to encourage others, I can't exempt me. I found myself getting in my comfort zone, something that I knew all too well. It almost had me defeated. I started feeling as if my goals were floating away from me. I was doing some general reading on how others shared their experiences on becoming an author. Some said it was hard trying to gain the exposure, or no one was interested in what he or she had to say. This made me feel some type of way. I wondered what would happen if no one wanted to listen to what I had to say. What if I couldn't encourage anyone else?

All of the fears and doubts invaded my mind, but then I remembered who I served. I learned I can't do anything without God in my life. He has prepared me for such a time as this. God said that He will line me up with the right people to help me get to where I need to be. Regardless of what I saw, I still believed in me. Being an entrepreneur has some strong challenges, but I know I can do it, and so can you. I don't care who is around you with an associates, bachelors or doctoral degree you can achieve anything you put your mind too. You can have any career you choose as long as you put the effort and time in it. Don't just sit there and think it is just going to come to you, trust me I tried. You may have to get some training here and there, speak to some people, enroll in some classes, but think about it; once you're done it is yours.

I know you are tired of me telling you to go after your dreams, but why not? What do you really have to lose: nothing? Stop being afraid of what others may say and stop listening to people who are telling you they wouldn't do this because of that. Believe it or not, people will try and stop you from going forward and make your idea theirs. They will take your career and put in the effort to make it work! I can remember someone telling me it would be hard for me because I am an African-American. Guess what? I believed what they were saying. I stopped pioneering myself for a little while because I felt as if she maybe was right, but God told me she was wrong. Regardless of what takes place just knowing that once everything is completed I can look back and say it was all worth it.

Here are my questions to you:

1. What steps have you taken to achieve your goals?
2. How are you overcoming the obstacles placed before you?
3. Are you surrounding yourself with positive people that inspire you?

Think on these for a minute. These are questions you should ask yourself daily, and doing so will help you monitor your progress.

Whatever you do don't give up. Write down what you feel is hindering you so you can improve. It will teach you more about yourself. By knowing yourself it will show you just how strong and determined you really are. Choose to make today a productive day for success. Try and forget about everything that is stressful in your life right now. Even better, act like you are the only one in this world. I have learned the less we worry about the more we can focus on greater things. When my mind is free, I am more creative, the juices begin to flow. This is what we need in order to process some things.

Sometimes we have so much going on, that we neglect ourselves. We are so busy fixing things that we don't realize our life needs repairing. I often sit back and wonder how I can improve my well-being? How can I provide a much better future for myself and my family? I know these are the questions you ask yourself daily. I must admit I am not at the place of contentment. There are bridges I still need to cross to say I am complete. My journey in finding a fulfilling career has been the hardest to date.

I have had so many letdowns, rejections and hurt in doing so, but I am still pressing my way and I pray you do the same. I will continue putting in every effort I can to show you that whatever you put your mind too you can achieve. If money is one of your hindrances don't let that stop you. There are other opportunities that will allow you to be your own boss if you don't have the money to start right away. There are many options available to help you toward a better future via entrepreneurship.

    I suggest you build upon the skills you already have. This may give you a quicker start especially by doing something you already have experience in. My goal is to see you all achieve greater. I can talk to you until I am blue in the face, but at the end of the day, this is your decision. I want to help you explore every option to help you on your journey. I didn't have that push when I was coming up and I tell you it is a blessing to have.

    When someone tells you they believe in you it is a great feeling and even greater motivation. It makes you believe in yourself a little more. Believing in yourself positions you for greater. Regardless of how long it takes, it is worth it in the end. Sometimes we give our self a time limit and when that time is up and nothing is completed we tend to give up or stray away. I too am guilty of this. Finally, I realized I needed to take the brakes off and keep rolling. Never give in to your tiredness because things will be left unattended. Refuel. Continue. Hard work equals results. If you need help don't be afraid to ask, you don't have to do it alone. I have come across many people who shared their success story with me on how they wanted independence and stability for their family. Make a commitment that today will be the day you begin your quest toward your dreams and goals.

    Let's not talk about it, let's be about it.

In trying to accomplish something you will find that it can be a bit of a hassle. It will even frustrate you to the point of quitting. When those times arise think about your reason for doing it. Remind yourself why this is important to you. You're headed in the right direction keep telling yourself that you can do it. Don't talk yourself out of the race, keep going you're almost to the finish line!

Reflection:

_____

_____

_____

Daily Dose: The Many Hats

   The reason I titled this entry "the many hats" is because some of us have so many in our closet that on some days we don't know which to put on. No, I am not talking about the physical hats we wear on our heads; I am talking about the entrepreneurial spirit we are all gifted with in one way or another. Some of us have so many talents that we don't know which to focus on. Instead, sometimes we focus on them all, but on different days.

      It would be great if we could manage each and every one, but who has the time? Some of us need more time than the other so when that starts happening it's going to become one of those hats that gets tossed in the back of the closet. Trust me. I know. I have a few! Sometimes it can be overwhelming because we want to use each one to the best of our ability. I am not saying you can't. I am saying I wouldn't want you to be stressed, or have mishaps because you are carrying too much of a load.

      The best way to decide is simply lean to more of the one that gives you definition and character. The hat that makes you feel good when you wear it. The hat you embrace that implements a lasting impression to anyone that comes in contact with you. In entrepreneurship, sometimes you find yourself puzzled on what direction you need to go in and when that happens sometimes we end up giving up because it seems as if it is too much of a hassle to pursue. I know within myself I have tried several different avenues that never went anywhere because I basically was doing too much.

      I had many things going at once, and there was no way I could focus. So if you are one of those that wear many hats and just not sure what outfit to match it up with let me give you some advice, how about get the hat that goes with everything something more of a neutral color that pairs well with your ensemble. In doing so it won't be stressful to manage. Trying to find your niche isn't so bad as long as you have some sense of direction. Gather your thoughts and move in the direction of your talents. Spend time trying on the one that you admire the most and are willing to rock in style. Trust me it will be the one to gain the most attention.

Sometimes it seems as if it is difficult to choose a career path due to you being skilled in so many areas. It just goes to show you are multi-talented, but don't let this cloud your judgment. Among all of your

talents lean toward the one you are willing to use the most. Usually this is the one that offers the most reward.

Reflection:

_____

_____

_____

_____

Daily Dose: Breaking Bread

As an entrepreneur, I found out that it is in your best interest to engage a mentor, because once you start traveling down this road, the journey can get very lonely. It can also wreak havoc on your mind and have you stressed out in more ways than one.

Being an entrepreneur has its advantages and disadvantages. Having a mentor or coach will be one of the best decisions you can ever make. Think about it, once you started on this path you had so many questions that needed answers, but you didn't know where to turn to seek them. Sure, of course you could drive to Barnes & Noble, visit the business section and grab a book that speaks on entrepreneurship, but there's nothing's better than having someone up close and personal to explain the concepts. There are so many avenues you can take to learn more about your mission. You can begin on social media with platforms such as LinkedIn to make the necessary connections.

This is a great platform to connect with individuals who have walked down the path you are traveling now. You can follow companies that may offer great advice from their articles. Twitter is another great platform. This will give you a chance to follow individuals who inspire you, friends who maintain a business, or companies that post motivational quotes to give you that extra boost needed. Facebook does the same, depending on how you use it. Try to find local events in your city take a friend and mingle. It is another great way to find out who is who, and who does what in your town. Be sure to bring networking cards and introduce yourself because you never know what someone is in need of. Building relationships can be rewarding. Sometimes it is all about who you know.

Meetup.com is a brilliant site that can be used in networking. It allows you to become part of a group and get to know your peers in the community. They also have events planned which get the individuals involved to network with one another. What better way to get exposure. I strongly feel every business owner has some sort of information which can help their fellow man. Joining together can do wonders for your community by bringing in opportunities. Regardless of your competitor, let's focus on helping each other grow and be successful in this economy. You can't survive in this world alone. After reading and realizing that having a mentor by your side isn't bad, or if you aren't quite sure of the idea just yet don't worry this information will always be available if you need it. Besides, what type of person would I be to give you a task without the instructions?

I have found that going through the local SCORE chapter in your area will allow you to find mentors who are ready to assist you in various fields. SCORE is a nonprofit association dedicated to helping small businesses get off the ground, grow and achieve their goals through education and mentorship. You can communicate with them by scheduling meetings or if you don't have the time for more of a sit down conversation they also give you the option of conversing by e-mail. Using the SCORE website will give you valuable information to better advise you on your search for a mentor.

You can find a mentor among your family and friends if you would like to connect with someone you know besides a stranger. Don't be bashful in making a visit to their location, but make sure they have the qualities you are looking for and the time to commit. There are many out there but have the open mind too that some may require a fee for their time. If you can afford it go for it at least then you will know they will be working it as a job than a volunteer. Take your time and research don't be in such a hurry but be motivated to step out of your comfort zone and ask for help. Others did it to get where they are today now it is your turn!

Connecting with other entrepreneurs makes this journey believable. They may have just the right words that you need to continue. Don't hesitate to get help if you need it everyone has a goal and that is to succeed. Get out there and seek resources to help your business mature you could be lending a helping hand in the process. Remember we learn from each other and what we learn can definitely help someone else in need.

Reflection:

_____

_____

_____

Daily Dose: How Professional Are You?

I find myself asking this question in many different situations each and every day.

I don't know everything and I am not a genius, but I understand the concept of professionalism. I have worked with a few people. Many of whom I would love to ask the question of how professional are you? In business, presentation is everything. It is important to carry yourself well, speak professionally and establish solid communication between your peers. Whether you are solo or on a team, there will always be some type of communication that will have to take place.

If you can't communicate with a team what makes you think you should network? Networking is the art of coming together with others to share ideas, build contacts and open yourself up to new ventures. You can't be secretive entering into the relationship thinking someone is going to steal your idea just because you shared your story. You have to trust. I know some will disagree, but I honestly believe each and every one has something that will benefit and help the other in the business world today. We might be in the same profession, but my mindset could be different than yours. I never get up tight when I am approached by a professional who is or aiming for the same profession as I am. I know who I am and what I bring to the table.

I am not in competition with you so I will not be sworn to secrecy. How can we work together if I am afraid to share certain information with you? The piece of information you are withholding might be what I need to move on a bit further. Remember, we have to network. I must continue to stress this on so many levels because this lack of communication is becoming a disease. The two major words I am addressing are networking and communication.

Sometimes, these words can make or break you if not done correctly. If you have a large corporation or business please understand you will have to establish a relationship with your team to make sure everyone knows and understands their role. If you do not establish those rules early you will develop major conflict among your peers. It will even separate your peers from you if you are not careful. If this sounds like you or if this is how you conduct your business, I have one word of advice – stop. This gets you nowhere, but a staff of angry individuals, a bad reputation and no community invitations.

When you are conducting business you must show professionalism to your customers, clients and staff at all times. Be mindful of how you speak and show less attitude as possible. There will be times when it appears that your employees or clients may express anger or frustration but you must never lose your composure. In order to continue servicing your clients or maintaining a relationship with those around you be professional, honest, and most importantly communicate.

Reflection:

_____

_____

_____

Daily Dose: Making an Impact

I remember speaking with an old friend from school, we spent the bulk of this conversation discussing our lives from past to present. I was surprised at her new mindset. It had changed drastically from being an honor student with a master's in business to being unemployed. She stated she moved away and started working in Corporate America for six years and after six years the company stated she was no longer needed.

She was always punctual and dependable. She did her job well, but her position was filled by someone younger – fresh out of college. They told her they were looking for fresh, new talent. Rather than the company informing her of their decision beforehand, they chose to keep this their secret and when the time had come – fill her position with someone younger. As you can imagine, this took a toll on her.

Since then, she has given up on going any further to accomplish her goals. This is something that happens each and every day in our society. You give your all to a company and sometimes it just isn't enough, but when it comes down to it, what do you do? You go forth with greater expectations, start working on becoming your own corporation, small business-and becoming the CEO of your life.

The same skills you gave to your job set them in motion for yourself. I strongly believe the best accomplishment you can have is when you invest in yourself. Even if you fail, at least you tried. I understand the fear of launching your own business, but instead of having that fear in your heart have the commitment to succeed within. This goes a long way. Regardless of what you are up against right now know that you have the authority to change your situation. If you don't like your job you can always find another, if you feel you don't get paid enough there is always one that pays more. You hold the key to your next accomplishment.

Have you ever applied for a job and they told you that you were overqualified? Instead of taking it as a letdown say to yourself it is their loss and maybe God didn't want you to have this position. If they couldn't appreciate the experiences you have then it wasn't the right opportunity for you. Pick up the pieces and move on. This company not hiring you did you a favor. Focus on your perfections. Build your own destiny. You want a career or job that will allow you to be the best and allow you to be rewarded for your hard work. That experience you have given the company you will always have it to take with you everywhere you go. If you want to reach higher heights, believe in yourself. Know that what you have on the inside of you can be used for the greater good. If no one else can see your potential, stand firm and build your foundation by making an impact in what you believe in, and that my friend is you!

Never let a disappointment separate you from your goals. Always remember when one door closes another one opens. Your gifts are too valuable to waste. Now is the time to invest in yourself and secure your future other than someone allowing you to secure theirs.

Reflection:

_____

_____

_____

Daily Dose: Threatened By Your Reflection

    Being threatened by our reflection is something that is so common everyone should be able to relate to it. It can prolong certain things from taking place in our lives as well as stepping out of our comfort zone or attending social events. It makes us compare ourselves to the next person and when we find our self not matching up we become intimidated. This reflection makes us feel uncomfortable. I struggled with this for a long time. This is one of the reasons why I was hesitant to try and achieve my goals. I thought I was not good or smart enough to pull it off.

    When opportunities to network with other business associates presented themselves, I would freeze and respectfully decline the offer. I was too busy cursing me that I painted a picture of me I didn't want anyone to see. One day, I was watching "The Talk" on CBS and they had been sharing their secrets all week. On this day it was Cheryl Underwood's turn and she shared about an opportunity that came about that she decided to give a try for the second time around.

    She was placed on a conference call to obtain more information. In doing so she overheard the young ladies talking about her wondering what she was going to bring to the table or why she was even chosen. She stated that they did not know she was on the line at the time and instead of hanging up she decided to stay on the muted call and continue listening. Even though things were said that were hurtful, she accepted it all for her personal growth. The one thing she said that stood out to me was even though she was bruised, she wasn't broken. This is a very profound statement because I can relate. It isn't always great words, or a pat on the back to help you get to your destination. Sometimes it is the ugly things that people say or do to you that will give you that extra boost of confidence you need to take the next steps. The next time you look at your reflection in the mirror, imagine the scars of hurt and not being accepted of feeling unworthy to know that the reason you couldn't see your glory was because you were looking at the wrong image. Take off the mask and reveal the beauty of the finished product. Say to your success, *"I did it!"*

If you allow fear to control your life it will hinder you from achieving your goals. Remind yourself that you have just as much to give as the next person. Regardless of who questions it you have to be confident in knowing that it is there. Everyone is blessed with different gifts so

now is the time to come out of hiding and reveal yours.

Reflection:

_____

_____

_____

Daily Dose: The Rain

As I was listening to the rain, I began wondering what if my blessings came pouring down repeatedly like rain drops, would I be thankful. Then I started realizing it actually does, but sometimes I didn't recognize it. Blessings are showered down each and every day I awaken. The reason why I don't realize it is because I am always looking for a specific thing. Some of us are looking for something more, but are not using what we already have. I was guilty of this at one point.

I wanted God to bless me with certain gifts, but why would He if I didn't glorify the ones I already had. It is funny sometimes how we want to be blessed with more money to buy a house, car or go on a vacation when we already have the tools to make it happen. Some of us would rather pay money to hear someone tell you the same thing you already know. Guilty as charged. I learned I could ask God for all these things to make me wealthy, rich and debt free, but couldn't trust myself to embark on what He has already given me. I found out that I was only setting myself up for failure. Knowing that if He would have blessed me with something else I would lose insight on what was before me.

Don't get me wrong, it was hard and a struggle, but only because I allowed it. That blessing God has stored up for you is yours. No one can take that away. Whatever your dream is to accomplish or be in this world start by making plans to see it through. Make yourself a to-do list every day that will help you in your steps of working on your blessing. You don't have to go any faster than you want too, but you do need to start at a comfortable pace. One thing that helped me was overcoming my fears. I was so fearful of doing something wrong that I never got a chance to see if I could do anything right. I had to constantly pray to be given strength and I had to encourage myself along the way.

I had to go thru some let downs and disappointments in order to make my dreams a reality. I had to turn away from some friends simply because where I wanted to go they felt as if the place did not exist. I am here to tell you that you are not going to have cheerleaders on every side. You are not always going to make a goal. You will miss a few shots here and there, but you must continue to aim and win.

Don't let your fear become a giant to overshadow you, let your determination overpower to make your fears disappear. I won't say there won't be any bumps in the road, but I can say once you cross it, the ride gets smoother. Don't just take my word, try it for yourself. Remember, you are your greatest fan, no one can take away your dream, but someone can always come up in your spotlight.

It is quite fine to want more in life but we must not fail to overlook the gifts that are already in our possession. Begin using what you already have to make room for more opportunities that will allow you to have greater.

Reflection:

_____

_____

_____

Daily Dose: Your Reliable Source

    Struggle is my word for today. Why, because my mind is a battlefield. I deal with consequences of decisions every day. The decisions of which way to turn, way to go, do I stay or quit? Those are the questions every entrepreneur faces daily. I knew that it wasn't going to be easy, but didn't know it was going to be this hard either. Sometimes I find myself questioning my ability as if I am unsure of what my talent is. I wonder if someone else sees something within me that I see in myself, but then I am reminded that regardless of what someone says I need to feel confident in myself.

    Nothing in life is going to be easy. I am afraid, yes even to the point where my stomach aches. I am tired of constantly fighting with my mind. I know some of you may think it really isn't that serious, but it is. Here's why. The reason is because this accomplishment is one I have always sought in life. I realized that my struggles will equip me, but they are designed to help others who may also be in this situation. It is hard to sit on your talents and not share them especially when you see that others are doing the same thing.

    Whenever I go to a book store the first thing I imagine is my book sitting there only being the last copy left or I imagine myself signing books for individuals who were touched in some way by what they read and who were inspired to go forth on their journey. I always wanted to help others in any way I could and completing this book is the first step I need to take, but the struggle is real. In our everyday lives, we need to encourage our self to go out and do bigger things. We really need to take the time to motivate our minds to continue in the direction that we were led whether it is spiritually,-or physically.

    We have to continue pushing regardless of the force that is in front of us. If I want to have a successful business I have to put in the effort in doing so regardless of the adversities, because no one is going to do it for me. Regardless of who isn't helping I need to know how to help myself. Even if I hear the word no one thousand times I just have to keep going until I get my one, "Yes." Sometimes, we run to others for confirmation on what we are doing, trying to make sure that what we are thinking of ourselves is matching up to someone else's standard.

    I don't know about you, but I am guilty of that. I wanted this feedback to give me that extra push, but guess what; sometimes you are not going to get it. I heard so many negative things in what I am trying to do, but I needed to realize that this is my goal, dream and life. It isn't what he or she states, it is what I believe. Yes, it gets harder by the day, but as the saying goes, *"Hard work pays off."* When you are looking for someone to pat you on the back, leave, turn around and go to that reliable source that knows you are capable, determined and focused. Let them know you have work to do. They will understand, because that reliable source is you. You know what your future holds so let's do it together.

We must realize if we don't encourage ourselves we won't move. If we don't put in the work we won't succeed. The only one who can destroy your mission is you. Focus on encouraging yourself to get to the place where you don't need to seek validation to continue your journey.

Reflection:

_____

_____

_____

Daily Dose: Time for a Change

How far would you go to make sure your family is financially stable? How many times have you said if I had more I would give them everything? Some of us have been saying these words for a long time. We even get depressed because we aren't able to provide for them as we feel we should. We go to work each and every day to punch the clock, but on payday when we look at our check it looks as if we weren't there.

We stay over countless hours to get paid overtime in hoping to see a difference within our check, but it makes us stay away from our family even longer. Our intentions are to make sure the house is kept, bills are paid, and our family is happy, but what about you? Are you happy? No. You are not simply because you feel as if you deserve so much more than what you are giving. You know you are putting in the time making sure you get to work, completing every task that is sent your way, but at the end of the day you are realizing you are working harder than what you are paid.

In these times, we all need some sort of income, but wouldn't it be so much better if it added up to what we bring home. Holidays come every year and we always say next year I am going to save and get "Michael" everything on his list. Then half way in the year you see it isn't possible from the numbers on your check or the hours cut from your job. What is your next move? Do you ask for a pay raise when 9 times out of 10 the answer is no? Do you ask for more overtime to continue missing your son's football games? All of these questions and thoughts run in our head on a constant basis where it begins to have us stressed out with the financial struggles.

I don't know about you, but I am tired of the rat race. I finally came to terms that I wanted better and to have it I had to work at it. There isn't anything wrong with a 9-to-5, but the issue occurs when this isn't enough. Look at yourself. You have so much potential. Work on ways to improve yourself and future. You owe it to yourself.

If you don't know where to start there is always someone out there who does. The one thing I always stress to people is that, there is something inside all of us that is special and unique. We were all placed here with talents & gifts to be used, but we have to understand it doesn't mean we can't use it for ourselves. There is nothing wrong with working for a company for 10 years, but how about starting a corporation of your own?

I know you're afraid, but remember God is with you. He will be the best business partner you will ever have. All you need to do is find your outlet, do some research, and go back to school to gather some training with a few classes. Check with your local Chamber of Commerce in your city. They may host workshops on business-networking opportunities. Look into business licenses, permits or even small business loans to accommodate you along the way. Help is available. You just have to seek it. Think about it once you go after something you really want, the reward is always greater. By doing so you may be able to spend more time with your family, attend your kids' activities and gather gifts one year ahead. Once you start living your dreams it will encourage your kids to embrace theirs as well. What are you waiting for? Go ahead. Get started. This is your season!

Change is a good thing especially when it comes toward your future. There are going to be times when in order to get what we want we will have to make some adjustments. So if that means coming out of our comfort zone, and entering into something new be excited this could be a major breakthrough!

Reflection:

_____

_____

_____

Daily Dose: What Do You See

Look in the mirror, and ask yourself if you like what you see? Even before you gazed in the mirror you already knew what your answer was. Just like everyone else, we all have something about ourselves that we would like to change whether it is our weight, how we talk, walk, or the color of our eyes. These matters should not require our time. Sometimes when we are told to elevate ourselves we end up looking at the outward appearance rather than the inner. The inside holds more valuables, hidden treasures that have yet to be seen.

If you would take the time to explore yourself, you would see all the possibilities that lie within you. Let me guess, you don't think you have what it takes? Well my question to you is how do you know if you have never tried? Sometimes it takes failing to know our strength. When you fail at something a lot of times the hurt and let downs become anger that boost up confidence to go head strong at that very thing you are looking to accomplish. The failure sometimes does something to our pride that causes us to react a certain way. For some it makes you go into hiding by being ashamed, and there are some that don't like to be looked at as a loss, but instead they pioneer their self to get back up and do greater which will allow that determination to come forth. How do I know? I have been there. I stopped a couple of times. I gave up. I became angry with no one other than myself.

The reason I was angry with myself is because I knew I could do it. It wasn't about what flaws I saw on the outside it was the beauty I knew I had on the inside. I finally got to the point where I realized that once I got past self I could focus on the issues that were more important. What I am trying to do is show you that there is so much more to you than your appearance, flaws, let downs and struggles. I want you to dwell on making a difference in your life by securing your future and bettering yourself financially, spiritually and mentally. Whenever you are already thinking negative when you glance at yourself you will never see anything positive. Yes, it is said, "The good will outweigh the bad," but in this situation it doesn't stand a chance, because you won't allow it. Let this be the day you start your journey to finding out what you would like your reflection to reveal. It will be worth it.

There is nothing greater than waking up to a brand new day and being comfortable about who and where you are. In life we have choices we must make each and every day. Why not let your choice enhance your quality of life and add security for you and your family. When I was growing up, I use to imagine what my life would be like wondering how many kids I would have, what my husband would be like, the places I would go on vacation, but the problem was I never factored in this thing called life. I didn't think about what I had to do to make any of these plans come true. I was just planning without a strategy. As I got older I realized I needed goals, goals that needed to be set in order for some things to happen in my adult life. No, it isn't easy, but it is a process. One of the main tools you need is yourself. You must be willing to devote the time in motivating yourself because you are the source that will open the door to determination.

The determination to succeed, conquer and jump over any obstacle that is placed in your path. There are times when I think what my life would have been like if I would have went against what I was told that wouldn't work, to see how successful I would be. Instead of going back in the past I moved toward the future and the same thing goes for you. It's never too late to finish what you started!

I know at some point you are thinking yes that sounds good and all, but where is the shortcut? How can I even program my mind to get on that level when I have so many more things to worry about? Honestly, there isn't an easy way. This is something you have to want more than anything, and that has to be an improvement within your life for the better. Don't just sit on your dreams, try expanding them and see what you come up with. Take a leap of faith. It will not cost you anything. It is free!

Determination is the key to your success it will help you overcome any obstacles that falls into your path or hinders you. Some people don't take entrepreneurship seriously. This is not someone who is trying to make a hustle. This is someone who is willing to take risks in laying down a foundation toward a better future. I have also learned that it can be challenging and enduring at times. Determination can take you a long way it has great benefits if you apply yourself. I realized that sometimes we don't have that drive we need simply because we have too many doubts.

We are constantly wondering what if this or that, before we even get anything started. That alone will stop you in your tracks. We must build ourselves up first and start taking steps while having the faith and determination to complete the mission. In conquering anything there has to be some motivation at hand, and a strong desire to get the job finished. If I didn't have this, you would not be reading any of my material because I would have talked myself out of this a long time ago. It has taken me years to get this far I had to push myself constantly, but I must say I am glad I did. I knew I wanted to be an author, but it wasn't going to happen overnight. I had to make time and sacrifices in doing so and I still continue to do so, but my strong will of determination encourages me to continue.

My desire is not best-selling status all I am looking for is for one person's life to be changed to follow their heart in pursing his or her dreams and who is willing to go the extra mile in securing his or her future. Finding that one person who will be able to motivate others by the determination they had in becoming who they are today and be willing to admit it is hard. So, think about what you are striving for and how much it means to you and go after it. Regardless of how long it takes keep that determination alive and I guarantee you will get to the finish line sooner than you think.

Never judge a book by its cover. Sometimes we surmise what the book is about by its cover without opening it to read the content. Sort of like how we treat ourselves. We focus on what we see on the outside and fail to see the potential we could have. Never take yourself for granted, if you would invest more time in yourself you will be surprised by what you may find.

Reflection:

_____

_____

_____

Daily Dose: Reality Check

Have you ever wondered what happened to the people who win lots of money from the lottery? Have you ever wondered what they do with it? Do they invest in anything or start a business? I constantly ask questions. Asking questions is not bad. The reason you question is to invoke your thought process. Honestly, I wonder. I know the first thing people usually think to pay off their bills which are a smart thing, but after you do this what else do you do? I have heard some say buy a house, pay off their bills, buy a new car, go on a shopping spree and all that good stuff, but what else? By the time you do all of this the money is gone!

Is this all you're working for let's say you quit your job in the process and now your money is thinning out. What are you going to do? You still have to eat, maintain that lavish home and car you purchased. Now, you have to go look for another job because you quit the one you had, and this time around you have to settle for less than your worth. If you're wondering where I am going with this, I am saying depositing that money in your dreams would have lasted longer. Sometimes, we have all the resources we need to better ourselves, but we use it all before we really even touch it. Not saying you have to spend all your money on a business just think of it as spending time in yourself. There is going to come a day when you are going to have to use what you have to get to where you need to be. The economy is getting worse, whether you believe it or not. You are going to have to know something because what we have or had for so long isn't going to be enough. No one is going to be impressed that you been on the job for 20 years until they decided to close their doors. They are going to want to know if you ventured out or did something on your own outside of that company. Because no one is available to speak for you, you will have to speak for yourself.

It is easy to get comfortable and not want to move because you did this for so long, but did you ever think longevity and succession. It is so hard for us to invest in our own dreams, but easy to pay to join someone else's. Sad, but so true we end up making someone else's dream prosper while ours dies. Sometimes, we have the audacity to give our opinion when we feel that it should be operated differently. My advice is to never complain on how someone else built their home when you're still staring at the foundation.

Thinking ahead and making smart moves can provide you with a solid platform for your future. Don't sit around and let your dreams crumble leaving you with regrets for a lifetime.

Reflection:

_____

_____

_____

Daily Dose: The Resolution

Do you really know how blessed you are? I am not talking about the car you drive or the house you live in I am speaking about the choices you have. You can be anything you want. Opportunities are abundant in your life. Knowing that I can be anything gives me something to look forward to. I think we sometimes take for granted the blessings that are in front of us. We look for other ways to enhance our lives through financial stability when the picture worth a thousand words is staring at us in the mirror.

As I ended 2015, I wanted to focus on creating real resolutions; those that remained. I stumbled and gave up a couple of times, but my determination kept me going. This country girl born in a small town had bigger hurdles she wanted to cross. Instead of being fearful, I tackled my fear with motivation, motivation to prove to myself that I can do anything my heart desired. I began my quest and I followed through until my mission was complete.

No, it doesn't stop here, but it puts me in a place where I am confident in reaching my next set of instructions on this path called Entrepreneurship. If it happened for me, it can for you, but you must first believe in yourself. Regardless of the struggle that comes along with it you have to think highly of yourself to continue. Everyone will not understand what you are doing, or where you are trying to go so you have to stay focused and know that this is your journey and sometimes you may have to travel alone. My advice to you is to never let anyone tell you that you can't do it or it will not work. That is the untruth because there have been many before you that are laying a solid foundation to help you achieve your goals. As long as you have faith there is nothing that you cannot accomplish. Why not start working on building a better you for a better tomorrow? The choice is yours. Don't delay.

The good thing about a new year is that it brings new opportunities, new mindsets and a chance to start over. This is your time to go hard at pursuing your goals. Don't let anything stand in your way or block you from having what you desire. If you want success go after it, the only thing stopping you is yourself. The opportunities are there. Will you pursue them?

Reflection:

_____

_____

_____

Daily Dose: Your Net Worth

One day I was surfing the net, researching some information on a celebrity. When her name appeared, I saw a link that indicated her net worth. I was completely blown away by the figures. I read up on her career outlook and discovered that she dropped out of school, but did a few gigs here and there that landed her on Reality TV. Now she is making six figures. Just reading the interview on her made me feel and immediately say, "Wow! Kim, you must get it together." Not that I am not, but in her becoming famous she just fought harder for what she wanted. She stated that she knew working for someone else would not amount to what she was worth.

She is doing awesome things in the community, sharing her experiences with others to show them that you can have anything you desire as long as you work hard for it. We look at different celebrities and imagine if our lives could be the same way. It can be if you are willing to put in the time and effort to do so. Nothing in life is easy at least from my viewpoint. Honestly if it were, I don't think I would want it. I would rather go through the ups and downs in becoming successful because of the lessons I would learn.

Not having patience will make you throw in the towel before anything gets started. If you want that freedom create a career goal and focus on it every day. Put in the time to work on having a more satisfying life and a great financial outlook. I know sometimes it seems hard to grasp, but trust me once you bring out that desire from a passion of yours nothing will stop you from taking steps forward. Celebrities are people just like us. We are all aiming for a similar goal and that is to be successful.

Let's not let our talents go to waste. Let's get on this journey so we can help someone else reveal their net worth. I don't know about you, but I would like to generate a six-figure salary. I strongly feel that once we see the big picture we will realize just how much we are missing out. We can't just sit back and wish we need to get out there and make it happen. The only reason why I am stressing this so much is because we all have been blessed with great gifts and creativity that can be used to have a successful future in knowing that we stepped out on faith, did the work and in return God blessed us abundantly!

You don't have to be a celebrity to have a great salary. What you need is to be willing to put in the extra work and dedication toward your career that it takes to get there. Celebrities experience similar failures and wins as we do. Without the internal motivation, commitment and drive, they wouldn't be where they are today.

Reflection:

_____

_____

_____

Daily Dose: Renew

Today, I decided to do a little writing instead of daydreaming about my desires and what it would be like to fulfill these dreams and goals. I realized the best thing to do was put my best foot forward and commit to putting in some action. Besides, who was going to do it for me? It is so funny how we are slothful, but yet want so much. I can't speak for everyone, but I know this applies to me. I thought to myself it is time to do some renewing of the mind on today. I needed to get some studying in to remind myself of what is needed to continue my career. One of the most important things I believe in is prayer.

You need strength to continue this journey, because every day there will be changes within your life to cause things not to move. You might have letters that need to be mailed, flyers given out or connections to be made. There is always something that we can be doing to better our self or business in some way. If you are in business for yourself, review your business plan to make sure you are moving forward as you desire. A lot of times we come up with a great idea and have a solid business plan. Some of you are already up and established, but in reading your plan you realized there are some things you haven't implemented. No need to worry. As a business owner, you can always make changes. That is what I call freedom knowing that I have the ability to correct my own mistake and errors.

I decided to do the same. Yes, I have a plan, but I started shifting a little to the left when I needed to shift to the right.

I realized that when you think you know and did it all there is always something you left out. If you are in the stages of building your business, this is where renewing your mind comes in. Start thinking on what you can do differently today than yesterday. Something that will benefit the business while putting you in a much more stable condition.

Today, I asked myself if I was giving it my all. Am I taking short cuts toward my future? No. I needed to work harder and tie up loose ends. I find myself wasting a lot of time. In business time is money. Yes, we have to have free time, but how much free time are we using? Is our life so grand that we have time to lie around? If you are like me the answer is no. We really don't, there are things we need to renew. Whether it is your mind or business, both can always stand improvement. Dust off your business plan, pull out that goal sheet. Begin doing some inventory. I promise you will find something in the books that needs to be replaced or added to.

In maintaining a lifestyle there is always room for improvement.

Reflection:

_____

_____

_____

Daily Dose: Which Way Are You Headed?

Have you ever felt as if you were backed into a corner surrounded by nothing but thoughts? Is your head filled with so many ideas that you don't know what to do with them? Even as you consider one, you realize 1,000 reasons exist as to why you can't do it. Your reasons dictate what is going on with you in the moment. You hear people say you are talented and smart, but at the end of the day you wonder why anything isn't happening in your life that lines up with this. You begin soul searching and realize those dreams, goals and ideas you had just didn't meet as of yet. So what do you do? Do you give up or strive once again? Is it tiring? Yes, but only because you have been around this block too many times.

When will it happen? What am I doing wrong? All of these questions running through your mind and the sad thing is you don't have an answer. Writing this book was hard for me because in the midst of writing I had to encourage myself to finish. I have started, stopped and started again for a long time. I felt as if I was going around in circles. Sometimes the change comes when you actually sit down and envision what it is you are seeking. I constantly have to remind myself of who is guiding me along this journey.

God has given me the ability to keep pressing my way until I cross the finish line. The best way I can help myself is by helping someone else. If my passion is in business, then I need to be assisting others to show them how to defeat the obstacles that may hinder them from taking that next step toward independence.

How can I help you? Am I pushing hard enough in my own fight to encourage you? Do I believe in myself enough to show you that you can do it? Well if I am not I would like to apologize because that means I need to try harder. One thing I have realized on my journey of being an entrepreneur is that there are some who have been there and did that, doesn't have an interest in sharing their struggles, encouragement or tips to help you succeed.

It doesn't speak for everyone, but there are some who fit the bill. Encouraging others helps me because I am one who believes when two touch & agree mighty things happen. Let's all keep pressing. Soon, all of this hard work will pay off. You control how high you go, if you don't put in the work you will always be at the bottom.

When you find yourself sinking start encouraging yourself to swim. You have come too far to get washed away.

Reflection:

_____

_____

_____

Daily Dose: The Beginning

It is now the beginning of 2016. We all know that at the beginning of the year we go back and forth in our resolutions that we set in the previous year. How many of you are actually sticking to it? Yes, I know 2016 is here, but a lot of us haven't even begun yet. No worries, you still have time, but there is no time like the present. Time waits for no one. Half of the year will be gone and some of you will still only be getting started. I know it all too well.

You may be wondering where you start well that's easy. Where do you see yourself in the next three to five years? Once you pin point that you can focus on it being your common goal. One easy way is to grab a personal journal where you can write down what you did each day. If that is working toward your goal you will be able to map out a lot of paths already crossed in hopes of getting to the finish line. I know you are thinking or wondering where this is going to get you, but I can tell you that you will get closer to the end of your journey.

Let 2016 be that year we make up for the previous years of where we started and stopped. At some point in time we need to complete those tasks if we ever want to achieve certain aspects within our lives. Last year, I learned so much in my struggle of being an entrepreneur that it has made me realize I was the issue not the problem. Yes, blaming everyone else was easy, but I had to come to the point where I stopped making excuses and playing the blame game.

Those games don't last long, and you will find yourself playing it alone. I was getting bored of the same old responses. That is right. The answers to each and every question were nothing because of my actions. Let me tell you, if you want to be successful in anything you do you have to continue and work at it. Determination is what's going to keep you encouraged to stay on that route. I can't stress enough how important it is to achieving his or her goals. These are all things that can help you for the better. Let's make 2016 the year of completion, no giving up, or going back let's move forward.

Going into business for yourself can be a nerve wrecking situation if it isn't completely thought out. To make sure the transition flows easily, believe in yourself and what you are doing so that you are able to pull it off. Remember, you can do whatever you put your mind too.

Reflection:

_____

_____

_____

Daily Dose: The Mission

Now that I have helped build your self-esteem, let's get to the good stuff. By now you should be in the process of building your empire. Laying down the foundation that will get you noticed. At this point, I am quite sure you had people who have filled your head with many negative things to make you question yourself or wonder if you made the right decision of becoming your own boss. Let me assure you are in the right place because you believed enough of yourself to take this long drive. You are going to hear the pros and cons, but that is alright because this is going to help you distinguish the good from the bad.

Now is the time that you let your haters be your motivators. Since your secret is out of the bag, why not continue spreading the word on the services you are offering? Building your clientele, while getting noticed the best way to get out there is to share with someone how you made it this far. One thing I realized is that there are people just like you and I that at some point in time felt as if it was impossible to go forth in this direction. When you come across the right person or people and they notice what you are doing it inspires them to work toward their goals as well. When building business relationships, it is important to learn from each other. There are valuable resources that can comply with whatever area you're in.

You can always brush up on some skills here and there to help you along. I have learned that the main thing to remember is patience. You can be anxious in your endeavors when the pace you're going is your starting point. That is why so many businesses fail because of less time preparing with not enough time to gather your thoughts followed by your plan. Having a business plan is a must just as well as having a long and short-term goal. Being an entrepreneur can be very rewarding if it's thoroughly processed, structured and implemented correctly.

Becoming your own boss is a big responsibility. It is a huge step. Congratulations to you for making this leap. You overcame many hurdles to get to this place. I am quite sure you fought against fear, doubt and yourself, but you won! Now is your time to put that hard work into motion.

Reflection:

_____

_____

_____

Daily Dose: The Spotlight

    By now, you should have an idea or a layout of what's to come. Now that you have convinced yourself you can handle your own weight. Now is the time to move further along and start reaping the benefits by being your own boss. You can begin gathering the business supplies you will need to start putting yourself on the market like investing in business cards, brochures and flyers. Something you can hand someone in passing if you don't have the time to sit and go into detail. I will admit advertising and marketing can be expensive, but in the end it is all worth it. Don't get me wrong there are some ways to get around it without paying a fee, but I stick by the saying, *"It takes money to make money."*

    Word of mouth advertising comes in handy, but it can also damage your reputation. We all know that everyone is not going to approve or agree with what you are doing. When it comes to building business relationships in retail or catering, everyone is looking for a sample or a way to compare your services to the next. Don't be afraid to give away something free. Don't think of it as losing; think of it as gaining a potential customer or client. You can set up booths to put your items on display so people can observe the product.

    Your business needs to reflect who you are. It is important that you represent yourself and highlight your business accordingly. Don't be afraid to ask around about prices regarding companies who are your competitors. People can come to you in hopes of finding a better deal. I would go even further like maybe wearing a business logo on a shirt or sleeve each time I step out so I can gain the exposure. It is no use having a business and no one knows about it. You can broadcast it on radio to local listeners. There is also social networking on the internet; e-mail marketing and you can also pay for leads. There are numerous ways you just need to devote in doing so. You can even host training seminars or events to gather people from all angles. Once you are in the media you are well on your way to gain new prospects.

In business, you should never get too comfortable when it comes to getting prospects to learn of your services. Just like the hard work, sweat and tears you went through in building put money into branding as well.

Reflection:

_____

_____

_____

Daily Dose: The Success

In this book, I am giving basic knowledge and useful information that is easy to digest. A lot of times you stumble upon books packed with information that will have you confused, forgetting keynotes or the whole concept of the book. I am trying to put it in the simplest form where anyone can understand. The reason I labeled this section as "the success" doesn't mean that this is the end. It means you conquered all the steps and answered all the questions. Fear and anxiety come along with it when you decide to do something different with your life and stick with it.

You should give yourself a pat on the back, you deserve it. This is also a part of your success. You should feel confident in yourself enough to take on the world. To know that you are trained in every area. Now you are in a place where you are in high demand. You know what you are doing and you're doing it well. Whatever position you are in is allowing you to help others service his or her needs, and on my behalf it feels great. Success isn't about how much money you make, it's the difference you made. You took the time to learn who you are, and what you are capable of achieving. Yes, there are many self-help books and tips to better yourself, but always remember you have the ability to bring forth all of the tools to create a mastermind. It starts in you. The books and tips provided are to enhance where you are.

When you come in contact with someone who has a desire or a passion, but who is also afraid to commit to the vision tell them your story and the result may surprise you. Making a difference in someone's life is a wonderful thing. You don't have to be a teacher or pastor to do so; all you have to be is a friend. This book is to motivate and capture something in you that can change your whole life and well-being.

Yes, you can be financially stable in your endeavors, but you can be at peace with how you got there. Enjoying what you do can help your business grow and your goals to operate more smoothly. You become more stable and functional in what you are presenting you won't be afraid to walk in your success. You will be able to place yourself among others and speak freely of your accomplishments. Once you get to this phase you can easily promote your services and know for sure that your clients will be satisfied not only in business, but also in their self-worth.

By writing this book, I am well confident in what I am describing to you because I also had to go through these steps to get to this phase in my life. I had to motivate myself to do so. If you are wondering if it was hard, the answer is yes. It took a lot of prayer and devotion to keep me traveling down this road and I must say it was worth it. It seems as if now is the time to make major decisions regarding your future. Especially the way the economy is set-up.

So many things are changing, sometimes it seems as if it is too much to grasp. This is why we must come up with a plan. A plan that is going to give us options, options that can provide backup. Now is the time to create a business plan or outline of your future. It isn't hard to complete. All you need are ideas and goals. You need to ask yourself what is my next step? How can I achieve this goal? Am I skilled in this area? These are questions that must be answered in your plan or outline. Let's not wait until something drastic happens before we make a move. Let's put in the work for it now! Don't be afraid, you will be surprised at what you can do or accomplish. To help you along I am going to include some questions to position you for the next level.

Congrats! You reached the end of my journal. I hope that you took down some mental notes and applied them toward your situations that you are dealing with while on this quest. As I mentioned before success isn't based on how much money is made, success can come from the mindset you gained or the courage to continue pursing your dreams. Hats off to you for taking the first step!

Reflection:

_____

_____

_____

Questions for Self-Evaluation

1. In your current position, do you feel as if you are getting paid your worth?

2. Do you enjoy what you are doing?

3. Do you see yourself in this position for the next five years?

4. Is this something you can retire from?

5. If you were to lose this position or the company closes, will you be able to support your financial needs?

If you answered "no" to any of these questions, now is the time to build yourself up from ground zero to a more established space. Investing in you may be a process, but it is a process with benefits. These benefits provide you more stability to your current lifestyle. I encourage you to take the time to learn who you are and the purpose you serve. Investing in yourself helps you become a better you, and a better you will help make a brighter future.

    I knew this wasn't going to be one of those large books crammed with so much information you were forced to choose between continuing to finish or scroll your Facebook newsfeed. I wanted to speak to situations we are faced with daily. I am confident anyone can take this information and use it within their life at some point.

    I want to see each and every one of you live a healthy non-stressful, successful life and I pray that my writings have encouraged you to do this and more. If you are still on board with me, I would like to share with you some information on how to continue building your empire and allowing it to run successfully within your business career.

    Once you start your business here are a few tasks you may need to jot down to make sure it is running correctly. Information that pertains to securing your business and its finances would be important to note. In securing your business & finances you need to make sure that you are going directly by your business and financial plans in order to get the results you desire for maximum sustainability and functionally.

A business plan is a detailed plan highlighting the objectives of a business, the strategy, plan to achieve them, and the expected profits. A financial plan is the devising of a program for the allocation and management of finances and capital through budgeting & investment. Having both of these plans are very important for the structure of your business. It helps you maintain up-to-date records concerning your financial properties allowing you to stay within your budget as well as keep track of your accomplishments and goals. Most small businesses fail to do so and usually end up in bankruptcy. Here are a few important things that can help you run a successful business.

1) Successfully meet the needs of your customers or clients, especially in the areas of customer service and support. Sometimes we tend to focus on our sales quota, as we should, but we should never neglect hearing from our clients and meeting their needs. If possible, giving a survey from time to time will allow business owners to know what he or she needs to improve.

2) Learn to build relationships and network with other business owners who may give insight or ideas that can help you along the way. There isn't anything wrong with getting advice from someone else who may be in the same field as you are.

3) Concentrate on your sales and marketing, create a marketing sales funnel system that will work for you and your business without hurting your finances. This needs to be a plan that will bring in repeated customers as well as attract new ones.

4) Hire a professional business coach to help you organize and guide you in the planning of your operation while offering business advice.

5) Spend more time growing your business. Take the time to gain more knowledge (you can never learn too much.) Investing time in your business will allow you to get more experience with ways on how to build a bigger empire. You will always find yourself coming up with solutions on making it better. Remember the sky is the limit. Not only do we have to focus on our finances, we also need to make sure we are networking properly. We may even have to ask ourselves questions like, do we feel that our business is growing? Has the number of customers or clientele increased or decreased within the last two years? Are you

getting the feedback you desire? If these questions have you wondering, then I think you can use a little help. I understand that establishing as well as keeping the business together can be tough.

    A business can be rewarding, and it can be your downfall if you do not invest in the right tools to keep it going. A lot of times what kills a business is lack of exposure. There are many businesses out here that have great products and services, but have never been heard of. I often hear many business owners say that advertising and marketing is very expensive. Every business owner should have a business card because you never know who you may run into that can use your service and what better way to introduce yourself than handing them a card. There are brochures you can use to add more detail on what you or your company has to offer. It will give you a chance to list more of your services while using your logo and other branding material. You can leave your brochures at your doctor's office or another place of business with permission to do so. People love to look at magazines or pamphlets while they are waiting. Make sure you have your name and contact number where you can be reached if someone is in need or interested in your services.

    Another way is to list an ad in your local newspaper. Millions of people invest in a daily paper, and you will be surprised at how many people actually take the time to read the classifieds. You can have promotional offers where you are giving away something half-off or free. Who would turn down something free? Sometimes people like to sample or try something before they buy it, but I know this isn't possible in all cases. You could host an event to introduce yourself as well as your business to the public. The main things you are trying to accomplish is getting noticed, socialize, and becoming acquainted with potential consumers. Websites such as Craigslist, allow you to post for free. Be careful while doing so using some of those sites will attract people who may not even be interested in the services.

    Last but not least, word-of-mouth. Many businesses operate on this level, but also beware you may receive negative feedback by someone who wasn't pleased with your service, and want to give you a bad name. In other words don't let this be the only way you advertise. Take the time to invest in your business with the proper tools that can give your business that extra boost it needs.

Here are a few social networking websites that can be used to accommodate your connections. These are just a few that can be used for different purposes, but there are many more you can research as well.

https://www.linkedin.com/
http://www.meetup.com/
https://www.facebook.com/
https://twitter.com/
https://www.youtube.com/
https://instagram.com/
https://www.pinterest.com/

There is so much information floating around that can suit any need you have.

As it pertains to your business ventures, your most valuable and reliable source is you. You can build up or tear yourself down. The choice is yours. Whatever choice you make, don't get caught up bashing someone else's vision when you operated in cowardice.

This is just the beginning of your journey that you and I will travel to moderate and empower while going after our dreams and goals. I pray that you will take heed to what you have read and pray for me to continue to provide more knowledge on this path we call entrepreneurship.

Acknowledgements

First, and foremost I thank God for depositing within me a desire to teach and help individuals find their way on a path of empowerment, personal well-being, knowledge and professionalism.

I'd like to thank my husband who has been there pushing me when I wanted to give up and believing in me 100%.

To my parents thank you for giving me life to become the warrior I am today.

To my brothers, thank you for showing me tough love with the support from the rest of my family and friends.

Last, but not least, to a wonderful pastor, (Pastor Vivian Troy) for the encouragement and teaching the Word of God that has got me this far to hold on and never give up. I have learned through God, anything is possible.

Finally, to you the reader, it is my prayer that you P.U.S.H., "pray until something happens." The entire concept of this book is to encourage individuals who have had the desire to achieve his or her dreams while allowing God to shift you in the right direction, all the while providing strength to overcome any obstacle set before you. I have written content that will position you in your daily steps while aiming for your goals in circumstances that dictates it won't happen, but you must always remember "WITH GOD ALL THINGS ARE POSSIBLE."

Regardless of what is going on in your everyday life you need to look at your storm, and say, "This too shall pass."

IF YOU HAVE A DREAM, LIVE IT. IF YOU HAVE A VISION, SEE IT. IF YOU HAVE A PLAN, DO IT. IF YOU HAVE A PURPOSE, FOLLOW IT.
-KGF

www.ingramcontent.com/pod-product-compliance
Lightning Source LLC
Chambersburg PA
CBHW070402190526
45169CB00003B/1071